TRUM

TRUMP RETURNS FOR 2025! :THE U.S. VS CHINA

- JEREMY STONE

JEREMY STONE

TABLE OF CONTENTS

WELCOMING CHINA INTO THE NEW WORLD ORDER

THE UNITED STATES CREATION OF COMMUNIST CHINA REVEALED

SKULL & BONES INFILTRATION OF CHINA

CHINA'S TRIADS & ILLUMINATI OF THE EAST

TRUMP RETURNS FOR 2025

THE U.S. DEEP STATE'S DEVELOPMENT OF CHINA'S EMERGING "ONE-WORLD GOVERNMENT"

THE "MADE IN CHINA 2025', "AGENDA 2030", AND PRESIDENT TRUMP'S 2025-2029 CONNECTION

TRUMP RETURNS FOR 2025

JEREMY STONE

Copyright © 2021 by Jeremy Stone Publishing, LLC All rights reserved.

This book or any portion thereof may not be reproduced or used in any manner whatsoever without the express written permission of the publisher except for the use of brief quotations in a book review.

Printed in the United States of America

9798727064733

First Printing, MARCH 2021

TRUMP RETURNS FOR 2025

TRUMP RETURNS

So, it came to pass during the staged five-year contractual world crisis that the winters became colder as the summers bore an unnaturally sweltering and relentless heat. Modified weather was no longer considered a conspiracy theory but an uninvited way of life. Truth was nowhere to be found, and news could only be gleaned by word of mouth and through rumor and speculation. Confusion abounded. World economies plummeted into oblivion as citizens went jobless and hungry under the newly realized Chinese One-World Governance and its New World

JEREMY STONE

Order. By 2024, what was left of trivial divergence and infighting between political parties gave way to a prevailing societal need for survival and mutual conviction that America and the rest of the world were robbed of what was once rightfully theirs; and that the West must now take it back. The Earth and the life of everything in it shrank as China shook the world.

Amid this carnage, once again, the world yearned for justice and the strong and steady hand of the previous President, and the delayed re-election of President Trump. The time to reclaim what we had all worked so hard for and had since been cheated out of by a corrupt and totalitarian World Government had come. If it meant total engagement of World War Three, the citizens of the world were ready to defend what was left of their freedoms. The injustices caused by World Government during the previous four years, by way of mass genocide, thought-

TRUMP RETURNS FOR 2025

control, and economic enslavement of the victimized citizens of the scammed world would no longer be overlooked nor tolerated. It was now the year 2024, Donald Trump was on the Presidential ballot, China had nearly taken it all, but the U.S. Military was still intact and would be the last recourse for a final global reclamation. Trump was set to sweep nearly all fifty states during the post-political climate of the times. Politics was dead, and the State-Sanctioned Global News Media and its fairy-tale distractions were now ignored altogether. The people were fully awake, engaged, and ready for justice.

WELCOMING CHINA INTO THE NEW WORLD ORDER

JEREMY STONE

"THERE LIES A SLEEPING GIANT. LET HIM SLEEP! FOR WHEN HE WAKES, HE WILL SHAKE THE WORLD."

~ NAPOLEON BONAPARTE, ON THE GLOBAL EMERGENCE OF CHINA

By the early 1970s, the world had already begun to feel the Earth shake as China emerged as a world superpower, awakening from its slumber. It had taken the U.S. 51 years, over half a century, 23 oppressive totalitarian leaders, the Chinese Government's transition into Communism, and a death toll of over 150 million Chinese citizens to address the "Sleeping Giant"; but by February 1972, the U.S. decided it was not too late to begin constructive dialogue with the

TRUMP RETURNS FOR 2025

emerging superpower, Communist China.

U.S. President Richard Nixon was scheduled to meet with the C.C.P. leader, Chairman Mao, as a necessary step to soften relations between countries and the Eastern and Western hemispheres of the world. No such feat had been attempted before, and the world watched in anticipation of what could set the tone for possible peace throughout the world for decades to come.

The tide had turned for the possibility of world peace as the Nixon/Mao meeting went off without a hitch. The cordial and open conversations between the two leaders and the placement of both U.S. and Chinese flags set side by side following the meeting proved to make what could only mean a meaningful and

JEREMY STONE

galvanizing meeting for the future between East and West; and with Nixon's unforgettable words, spoken thereafter: "We have at times in the past been enemies. We have great differences today. What brings us together is that we have common 'interests which transcend those differences...And so let us, in these next five days, start a long march together. What legacy shall we leave our children? Are they destined to die for the hatreds which have plagued the Old World? Or are they destined to live because we had the vision to build a New World?", there could be no disputing the fact that progress was indeed made between the U.S. and China, and an enduring alliance was forever established.

The impossible partnership between Capitalism and Communism was formed as the Gods looked down with glee as an eternal world peace and a welcomed

TRUMP RETURNS FOR 2025

addition to the New World Order (China) was realized. This was the official narrative promulgated by the Global State-Run Media as the absolute truth about a peaceful and harmonious world, where differences in Communist and Capitalist societies could easily be overlooked with one simple conversation; Not to mention the Western world's ability to easily ignore China's recent genocidal atrocities of over 55 million dying from starvation during the famine of the 'Great Leap Forward' - all glossed over seamlessly during the meeting. All of the horrors committed by the C.C.P. were now resolved as China had suddenly become a welcomed new member of our peaceful New World Order; Now that the foundation had been laid for a lasting world peace was miraculously established between East and West, World peace was a real possibility now, and the peoples of the world exhaled a universal sigh of relief as

JEREMY STONE

another possible World War had been averted. This was the official story, which was propagandized by the New World Order to be written in every history book as gospel truth for the masses, but was the world too blind to notice it was being told a fairy tale?

The true hidden history of relations between China and the U.S. began just around the time America was establishing itself as a Sovereign country during the American Revolution. While the Illuminati was at work infiltrating the United States Government in the 1770s, the Chinese Illuminati was simultaneously busy infiltrating and warring with China's free Nation-State, then ruled by the Qing Dynasty. It took the American and British Shadow Governments over a century to overthrow the Independent State of China, which was by the late 1700's just a sleeping giant minding its own business and wanted nothing to do with a

TRUMP RETURNS FOR 2025

Communist form of Government. Still, Communism is precisely what the West gave them. China's C.C.P. was a creation of an American/British operation which was formed on Jul 23, 1921. Once assembled, the political party was immediately met with heavy resistance, first from Japan's controlled opposition, as the C.C.P. was set on completing its overthrow of the Chinese Government. Even then, the United States openly supported the Communist regime, forcing Japan to surrender to Communist China. Civil War quickly ensued between China's citizens and China's Communist Party against the Totalitarian regime. Still, by 1945 (An unlikely so-called coincidental date coinciding with the end of World War II), the C.C.P. had established itself as the official Government of China. A phony Cold War followed between the U.S. and China—fully coordinated between both sides, and by the time Nixon showed up for "peace talks" with Mao Zedong and

JEREMY STONE

Primer Zhou Enlai in 1972, the carefully choreographed charade had finally come to a close; In short, the Chinese Government we recognize today is nothing more than the 'Eastern Illuminati.'

During this staged televised meeting, most never knew that Chairman Mao had, in fact, already been an active member of Skull and Bones, A.K.A Yale in China since 1921 and was in full cooperation with the United States and the New World

TRUMP RETURNS FOR 2025

Order's agenda decades before the 1972 "peace talks"/Nixon-Mao Summit.

What is the correlation between the "Made in China 2025" Agenda, the U.N.'s

"Agenda 2030", the Presidency of 2025-2028, and the "Sleeping Giant," China's economic and technological emergence and dominance over the world VS the established American/Western Military dominance? What are its implications for the world during this critical time in history?

JEREMY STONE

Is it possible that Gog and Magog hold symbolic and literal meanings, where the two remaining Giants/Superpowers over Global Military/Industry portend the inevitability of events to come for 2025 and beyond?

How much economic and societal dominance will China have established over the world during the next four years, and is it even possible for the U.S. and the world to reestablish and recover from by 2025?

Is there valid proof that Communist China is a creation of the American Deep State?

Did the U.S. and United Nations intentionally give China temporary power over the New World Order decades in advance, just for future Presidents to deal

TRUMP RETURNS FOR 2025

with and clean up the mess for in the future?

Has intense conflict, building up to a possible Third World War between the United States and China, been planned by the elite 100 years in advance?

Will Trump return for the final showdown between China's totalitarian State and the United States of America?

All of these questions and more will be answered to prove how and why Trump returns for 2025 is an inevitability.

"I think this would be the time (for Obama to strike a financial deal with China) because we really need to bring

JEREMY STONE

China into the creation of the New World Order, the Financial World Order." - **George Soros**

"There is no doubt China has become an easier place to do business. When you think about what has happened over the last ten years, let alone 20 years, it is an achievement beyond recognition… I think we all have to move to the opportunity of having the Chinese Yuan convertible with other world currencies, but the challenge also is whether we should move to an international currency." - **Evelyn De Rothschild**

"We have to give credit to President Nixon, and Henry Kissinger's initiative broke the ice. They did - but they confronted a residue of suspicion, & that suspicion was mutual, and

TRUMP RETURNS FOR 2025

grievances also mutual. And it really took time for the relationship to become more normal, more predictable, and eventually, they became open - and in fact, initiated a kind of <u>secret collaboration or alliance</u>."

- Zbigniew Brzezinski

"<u>But there really are issues of the construction of a New World Order. That is what this is about - And that is the sort of dialogue the Chinese are generally good at.</u> And so, a partnership between us is essential. A conflict between us is going to exhaust us both in tactical exercises; it cannot be conclusive<u>. The New World Order has to satisfy both (the United States and China)</u> otherwise - it will lead to tensions -that will exhaust us both."

- Henry Kissinger

JEREMY STONE

The developing coherence of Asian regional thinking is reflected in a disposition to consider problems and loyalties in regional terms, and to evolve regional approaches to development needs and to <u>the evolution of a New World Order</u>."
- Richard Nixon, 1967

"And the hope that each of us has to <u>build a New World Order</u> – **Excerpt from President Nixon's Speech in Peking, China, 1972**

If you are reading this, chances are you are already somewhat familiar with my previous five books dealing with the interlock and the long-detailed history of the development of the global criminal cabal; Shadow Government, Deep State,

TRUMP RETURNS FOR 2025

4th Reich, International Enterprise, and now the introduction of the term I like to call "Red Corporatism"– which should now be simply referred to as the "New World Order." I have substituted the phrase "Corporatism" for "Capitalism" since the connotations of the often overused "Red Capitalism" gives the deliberate false impression that the "Capitalism" we understand in the West could somehow be associated with Communism. The New World Order and One-World Government, which is now on the verge of completion, is a CRIMINAL INTERNATIONAL SOCIALIST AND COMMUNIST CORPORATION BUILT FOR THE ELITE. Our once American form of Capitalism for the American people is now being eroded at an alarming rate and being replaced by a handful of Chinese Controlled Monopolies, "Big Tech," "Big Pharma," and Corporations; otherwise, now known as "Red Corporatism."

JEREMY STONE

This form of Red Corporatism, wherein China has been built up to now control over 90 percent of the world's vast resources, surprisingly, is not new. Instead, the 'Opium Wars' of 1839 and 1856 paradoxically opened the door to China's later rise to the ranks of a world superpower. The agreements and treaties between Great Britain and China were designed to bolster China into the New World Order for the future.

The Opium Wars began in 1839 with the First Opium War, ending just a few years later in 1942. The Qing Dynasty Governing China would not concede, even after its port cities along its coasts and rivers were pummeled. The relentless and ruthless superiority of the Naval forces of Great Britain proved to be effective in destroying everything in its path. Despite China's three years of destruction and

TRUMP RETURNS FOR 2025

humiliation, China refused to relent to the British Empire's imperialist superpower. In 1856 Britain returned for the Second Opium War with China, this time with the aid of its military ally, France. By this time, the advancements in British ships and artillery were twice as destructive, and the Qing Dynasty must have realized they were up against more than the British. They were fighting the New World. While China did not surrender, they agreed to sign the "Unequal Treaty," which would force the British trade of Opium upon the Chinese people and imposition a sixty percent tax on all of its exports.

Why were these wars between Great Britain and China called Opium Wars? This name may give a surface-level impression that the British were attempting to thwart China's production and exportation of its Opium when nothing could be further from the truth. The "Opium Wars" were merely the result of the despotic and ruthless Corporatist Superpower of Great Britain used a secret army of Chinese, smuggled silently through China's borders to hook the Chinese people on the highly addictive drug known as Opium; after addicting millions of the Chinese population on this powerful drug, the British then proceeded to sell and trade it back to them for unbelievable profits. The secret army Britain used to turn China into a society of opium addicts were known in China as the 'Triads,' also known as the Illuminati of the East. These Triads were hard at work hooking China up on Opium a century before the "Opium Wars" between the British and China even began in 1839.

TRUMP RETURNS FOR 2025

In the 1600's these 'Triads' were Corporate and High-Level Freemasons, and it took them over 100 years of illegally utilizing this process of addicting China on Opiates, then profiting from the trade of Opium back into China; until finally, China was forced to stop all imports from Great Britain and Europe altogether. The drug-dealing Imperialists of Europe would not hear of it and immediately resorted to restoring its 'Opium Trade' by invading China's Qing Dynasty. The build-up to the British/Chinese "Opium Wars" was also planned over 100 years ahead of time by Masons' secret society who infiltrated China. A Century later, this elite group morphed into yet another new and more exclusive secret society in China, remarkably similar to a 'Chinese Mafia.' This was and still is the most elite club globally, formed in China, England, and America simultaneously in 1832; Skull & Bones.

China had an adequate and sizable population for Military expansion and had invented gun powder in the 13th century, long before the British knew what it was or how to use it. Gun Powder was readily available to the Chinese people, and the weaponry used by the Chinese and British, at that time, held no considerable advantage, one over the other. The British

TRUMP RETURNS FOR 2025

had four distinct advantages over China during the Opium Wars: They had successfully addicted the Chinese population to the highly addictive drug, Opium; The British were decimating the Chinese Economy and the successful infiltration of Skull and Bones into China over a period of 100 years.

JEREMY STONE

The one advantage China had over the British was their colossal population density, which would mean that although the British could ravage most of China's port cities, they could never station themselves in China to monitor and Govern China's Qing Dynasty without quickly being defeated. The British knew they could only slowly wear down the land of the Dragon through the destruction of its port cities, drug-pushing, flooding its markets, and decimating its population.

The British Empire did not force China to sign "The Unequal Treaty," ending the Chinese/European Opium War in 1860. Instead, what appeared to be the surrender of the Qing Dynasty was simply the collaborative staged effort between the Eastern and Western Societies of Skull and Bones; all of which were established, not coincidentally, in America, Great Britain, and China simultaneously in January 1832.

TRUMP RETURNS FOR 2025

SKULL & BONES IN CHINA

According to Joseph Brewda's publication, Bush's China Policy- "Skull & Bones": "Skull and Bones is a secret fraternity at Yale University which is restricted to a mere fifteen student members per year. The society was formed in 1832 by General William Russell, whose shipping firm later dominated the U.S. side of the China opium trade. Yale University was founded by Eli Yale, who made his fortune working for the opium smuggling British East India Company. Skull and Bones became the recruiting grounds and preserve of the most important New England-centered families- families who also made their money in the opium trade. These families, whose sons regularly join Skull and Bones, include the little-known but powerful, Coffins, Sloanes, Tafts, Bundys, Paynes, Whitneys. They are a dominant element of

JEREMY STONE

the U.S. 'Eastern Establishment' to this day. The Bush family is one of a cluster of lower-level Establishment families controlled by these interests."

Skull and Bones is generally regarded as one of the most powerful Secret Societies within World Government hierarchies. What has not been made clear is that its founding members and their elitist families set up this 'Fraternal Order' with the goal to build a United 'Red Corporatist' One-World Government. This New World Governance system was orchestrated for one reason and one purpose only; to rapidly bolster Communist China as the dominant global superpower for the world's countries to collectively reshape their respective Governments after - for the completion of the New World Order.

TRUMP RETURNS FOR 2025

"<u>Out of the renaissance spirit now existing in China</u>, it is possible, if foreign nations can be prevented from wreaking havoc, <u>to develop a new civilization better than any that the world has yet known</u>."
-- Lord Bertrand Russel, 1920

Lord Russell goes on to say that on:

"Jan 19, 1832 - An obscure secret society known as "Skull and Bones" may have more to do with George Bush's obsessive support of Beijing's mass murderers than one may think."

Once the trade and Opium Wars between Britain and China were settled in 1860, the real Globalist meddling began later in 1898, when Britain prepared a secret contract with China, promising to return Hong Kong to the people of China in 100 years. This contract was honored in 1997, unbeknownst to the world, that Hong Kong's freedom from Imperialist

JEREMY STONE

Britain was pre-staged 100 years prior for the advancement of China's coming New World Order.

"George Bush, the first U.S. diplomatic representative to the People's Republic of China back in 1973, was a member of Skull and Bones. So were his father, brother, son, uncle, nephew, and several cousins. Winston Lord, the Reagan-Bush administration Ambassador to China, was a member; so were his father and several other relatives. James Lilley, the current Ambassador to China, was a member of Skull and Bones, as was his brother. Except during the Carter administration, every U.S. Ambassador to Beijing since Kissinger's deal with Mao Zedong was a member of the same tiny Yale cult. A mere coincidence ?"

TRUMP RETURNS FOR 2025

"It has since been shown that 'Yale in China' was an intelligence network whose purpose was to destroy the republican movement of Sun Yat-sen on behalf of the Anglo-American Establishment. The Anglo-American "Establishment" hated Sun because he wanted to develop China. On the other hand, they loved the Chinese communists because they intended to

"MAO WAS A YALIE – Back in 1903, Yale Divinity School established a number of schools and hospitals throughout China that were collectively known as 'Yale in China.'"

From the New Federalist, January 1996

JEREMY STONE

keep China backward and were committed to growing dope. One of 'Yale in China's most important students was Mao Zedong."

-- The New Federalist, January 1996, "Bush's China Policy: Skull & Bones"

For some, the idea of an invasion of both the United States via the Western Illuminati and China via its Eastern Illuminati may be difficult to accept. However, it is a hard truth that we must confront if we are going to tackle this problem head-on properly when President Trump returns for 2025. Just as the Illuminati of the East infiltrated China over 200 years ago, so was the United States, by the British Empire of the Western Illuminati. This effort in which the U.S. was first formed as a Capitalist country to be later subverted into a 'Socialist Nation' has been carefully choreographed over two and half

TRUMP RETURNS FOR 2025

centuries. As the British Imperialists (Western Illuminati) infiltrated the United States, the Eastern Illuminati were busy simultaneously infiltrating China and the Qing Dynasty with the same groups and Secret Societies; The Illuminati and Skull & Bones. Without examining all of the pieces of the puzzle as a whole, it is easy to point the finger at Germany (also instrumental in transforming Europe and the United States into Socialism with its 3rd and 4th Reich's), Israel, and particularly the Vatican (which does have a history extending though time with its Roman Empire and 'Papal States'; but upon closer investigation of our true world history, it is should be clear that Britain and it's Manifest Destiny' British Empire are the true societal meddles who rule our world. The Imperialist British have decided which country gets power over the other, and for now, their New World Order and One-World Government have been handed to China.

JEREMY STONE

CHINA'S TRIADS

China's Triads are essentially what started as the Secret Society (China's Illuminati), which the British Empire (and its shadow-controlled partner, the United States) used to overthrow China with its opium trade; and over a period of hundreds of years, eventually created the Communist China we know today. Over time, these 'Chinese Triads" gradually morphed into what is today, undoubtedly, the most powerful organized crime family, with is centrally based in China, but with units that span the world. Ironically, today these ruthless gangs, which once brought down the Qing Dynasty, now only serve the C.C.P.'s criminal and Red Corporate criminal activities.

TRUMP RETURNS FOR 2025

These Chinese gangs are based in Hong Kong and are the unofficial and underground police force for the Communist Party of China (C.C.P.). Their criminal corporate endeavors are primarily based on money laundering, drug-dealing (heroin trafficking), and child prostitution. Its heroin/opiate trafficking operation. The private partnership between the Triads and the high-level Freemasons worldwide is a critical factor in keeping their heroin trade a thriving international criminal enterprise. The Golden Triangle is triangular since it borders three adjacent countries; Laos, Thailand, and Myanmar. The territory covers a perimeter 366 thousand square miles wide and is responsible for the world's largest exportation of methamphetamine worldwide, amounting to over 140 tons of smack annually. This illicit and silent drug operation does not even include China's Opium production and trade, which is still continually active

JEREMY STONE

as the second-largest exporter of Opium throughout the world, especially in the United States, Great Britain, Canada, and Australia. All told, China produces more illicit drugs, illegal and pharmaceutical, than any country in the world.

According to Canada's former diplomat to Hong Kong, now turned whistleblower Brian McAdam: "Within each Chinese community, there's usually a strong Triad presence controlling and extorting money from the businesses, and if there's drugs, they're bringing them in."

Also assisting these Triads are the C.C.P.'s top-level hierarchy of the Triads, known as 'Dragon Heads', which are centrally based in Hong Kong. The Dragon heads are the middlemen between the C.C.P. and Triads, who help these triad groups front and create so-called "upstanding businesses" keep the

TRUMP RETURNS FOR 2025

appearance of a clean operation in China. The majority of these State-Sponsored front Red Corporate organizations reside in and around Shanghai, which continues to flourish with yet more cover from some of the region's wealthiest moguls.

"'The Triads are the most powerful criminal fraternal group in the world, except for the Illuminati and the families that make up the Illuminati's Committee of 300. The Mafia Is small peanuts compared to the Triads. The Triads are almost untouchable by any law enforcement group. For instance, in Great Britain, the British do not have hardly any ethnic Chinese on their police force to even try infiltrating the Triads." -- **Fritz Springmeier**

JEREMY STONE
YALE IN CHINA

"William F. Buckley was not the only Yale figure connected with the Presidential trip to China. Without Yale's support, Mao Tse Tung may have never risen from obscurity to command China. Jonathan Spence was the first to discover Mao-Tse-Tung's connection with Yale. The Professor noted, "In 1919 Mao, aged 26, was in Changsa, having finished his middle school education,

TRUMP RETURNS FOR 2025

He visited Peking and, while there, received his serious introduction to communist theory in Li Ta-Chao's Marxist Study Group. Now, if he was to develop a reputation in socialist circles, he had to find a forum to propagate his views... At this crucial point, the student union of Yale-in-China invited Mao to take over the editorship of their journal. Mao accepted the position and changed the format of the student magazine: it would now deal with social criticism and current problems and focus on "thought reorientation."

–Yale Daily News No. 96, September 1972, Yale Digital Library.

Yale in China was activated first by the Triads (The Eastern Illuminati), then later consummated by the United States Government's O.S.S., or the Office of Strategic Services (precursor to the C.I.A.)

JEREMY STONE

during World War II, for the express purpose of permanently embedding the Communist Chinese Government (C.C.P.) into China. Between 1941 and 1949, 'Yale in China' was directed by George Bush's close relatives and Skull & Bones associates, Reuben Holden and Bill Donovan, where the O.S.S. trained China's guerillas and Triads for their coming Communist takeover of China.

In "The New Federalist," "Bush's China Policy, Skull & Bones," dated January 1990, the true, behind-the-scenes relationship between the United States and China's C.C.P. New World Order is exposed: "George Bush, the first U.S. diplomatic representative to the People's Republic of China back in 1973, was a member of Skull and Bones. So were his father, brother, son, uncle, nephew, and several cousins. Winston Lord, the Reagan-Bush administration Ambassador to China, was a member; so were his father and several other relatives. James

TRUMP RETURNS FOR 2025

Lilley, the current Ambassador to China, was a member of Skull and Bones, as was his brother. Except during the Carter administration, every U.S. Ambassador to Beijing since Kissinger's deal with Mao Zedong was a member of the same tiny Yale cult. A mere coincidence? The Anglo-American "Establishment" hated Sun because he wanted to develop China. On the other hand, they loved the Chinese communists because they intended to keep China backward and were committed to growing dope. One of 'Yale in China's most important students was Mao Zedong. 'Yale in China' was also strongly associated with the New York-based Union Theological Seminary, which has been a center for U.S. subversion of Asia (literal wolves in sheep's clothing). Every prominent radical leader operating in Korea today, for example, was trained at Union Theological. Union Theological was dominated for twenty years by Henry Sloane Coffin, a U.S. intelligence executive

JEREMY STONE

from the Sloane and Coffin families. He was a Skull and Bones member, as were a dozen of his relatives."

Wang Hao, upon overhearing the secret meeting between David Rockefeller (Godfather of the New World Order) and Mao's 3rd party diplomat, Zhou Enla, noted: "(That) when meeting David Rockefeller, Zhou said to him that it was necessary to find appropriate methods conducive to *the development of the trade between two sides under different political systems.*"

Although the Gold Standard was "temporarily suspended" several times during the course of American history, right before the Civil War, in 1861, then again when President Theodore Roosevelt sold out America to the elitist crook, J.P. Morgan, and his Illuminati "Banksters in 1913, and again, as Socialist Nazi

TRUMP RETURNS FOR 2025

Collaborator, F.D.R. dissolved the U.S. Constitution (See "The New World Order"), initiating the beginning of the Socialist Corporate 'New World Order' in America; However, the U.S. Gold standard was not "permanently suspended" until President Nixon sold out the American Economy to China, in 1971, paving the way for today's China-Dominant Communist One-World Governance.

While America dominated the world economy, making use of its currency backed by Gold and Silver for nearly 200 years (wherein the late 1870s, we could exchange 20 dollars for one ounce of Gold), by 1971, a secret Communist/Capitalist economic merger and the beginnings of a 'China-Dominated' New World Order had begun. Not only had the gold-standard been permanently suspended and replaced with fiat paper money, but what was left of American gold reserves were being

JEREMY STONE

covertly shipped to China. After Nixon suspended the Gold Standard, the American public began suspecting that Fort Knox may not hold the 8,100 tons and 300 Billion dollars' worth of Gold that the U.S. Treasury claimed it contained. By 1974 a staged inspection by the U.S. Congress followed. The "Gold" found in Fort Knox was far lighter than real Gold and was hastily covered with a thin layer of superficial gold-plated coating. Once fortifying the American Economy, the Gold Bullion, located at Fort Knox, had since silently been cleaned out and sold to China for pennies on the dollar via the Bank of London.

While President Nixon permanently suspended the United States Gold Standard, it should come as no surprise that China's gold reserves and repositories have since grown over the last fifty years, from non-existent, in 1971 (the U.S. Gold Standard Suspension) to what

TRUMP RETURNS FOR 2025

is now estimated to be as large as 1,000,000 metric tons! While an American

JEREMY STONE

Gold Standard suspension was being finalized, the Chinese C.C.P. was amassing its newly cheaply acquired Western Capitalist Gold, coupled with its own for the build-up of a 'Gold Repository' that is expected to become so vast in the years to come that it could easily supply the world with its new currency, or "Digital Yuan" backed by this Gold. In fact, China has been talking about its move to set a Gold Standard for the Chinese Yuan for some time now, and this should not be perceived as idle rhetoric since they have now accumulated and stolen more than enough Gold to do it.

What would be the implications of a Chinese currency (the Yuan) being formally announced as being fully backed by Gold in a world where all the other countries continue to use fiat paper money? To put this very real scenario into perspective, the effect of a gold-backed Chinese currency would make our current plandemic's Great Depression look like a

TRUMP RETURNS FOR 2025

minor recession, and the fiat-based paper money currencies of the world would become absolutely worthless against a 'Gold-Backed Yuan' overnight. Without any value in the remaining countries' currencies fiat-based paper money, the 'Gold-Backed Digital Yuan' would quickly become the only choice for those countries of the world to accept – by force. This is exactly what the newly established Chinese New World Order and its build-up are all about, forcing the World's Nations to beg for its international One-World Currency, backed by Gold, or starve in resisting it. The Rockefeller's Trilateralist 'Group of 30" have organized and established direct links to the Central Banksters of the World, including China's previous Central Bank President, Zhao Xiao-Chuan -- who have been secretly collaborating, plotting, and planning for a future New World/China-based, One-World-Government currency since 1979!

JEREMY STONE

The plandemic is nothing more than a 5-year contract (See my book, "Surviving the New World Order" for more details surrounding this five-year contract) which has been agreed to by the nations of the world to expire in 2025, once completed. Not coincidentally, this is also the year the "'Made-In-China" agenda is expected to ramp up until its deadline, which is set to complete by the year 2025; Also, not coincidentally, this is also directly correlated with the same four-year term in which Trump is scheduled to return and to be sworn in as President in 2025, where the ultimate showdown between the U.S. versus China is set to begin.

TRUMP RETURNS FOR 2025

The purchasing power of $1 from the time the Federal Reserve was established in 1913

1933: FDR suspends gold convertibility; makes gold illegal for U.S. citizens to own

1971: Nixon suspends Bretton Woods gold-exchange system

The dollar has lost 96% of its value since 1913

Source: BLS CPI Data

JEREMY STONE
U.S. DEEP STATE DEVELOPMENT OF CHINA'S EMERGING "ONE-WORLD GOVERNMENT

CHINA'S NEW WORLD ECONOMY

China's Economy has grown consistently at a staggering rate **of** 19 percent annually from 2008 through 2013, and with the recently installed administration with a burgeoning global W.E.F. "Great Reset," China's economic growth will only continue to accelerate at an exceedingly alarming rate; as it approaches its complete domination over the world's Economy. China has already outperformed Europe and the United States with trade throughout Asia, South America, and Africa, dominating the petroleum, mineral, and energy markets of Iran, Saudi Arabia, Venezuela, and Sudan.

TRUMP RETURNS FOR 2025

China's role within the New World Order lies in its acquisition and control over the world's natural resources, giving them the leverage necessary to forge global alliances, corporate mergers, and lucrative partnerships (i.e., scamdemic contracts) between nations. China has been methodically buying out the corporate New World for over half a century, transferring hundreds of billions of dollars to corrupt officials, U.S. politicians, lobbyists, and the C.E.O's running our internationalist cabal, yet nothing has been done about it.

China's production and trade are also increasing exponentially throughout the U.S. and Europe (with the exception of the years 2017-2020, during the Trump administration), the United States and the West have remained stagnant with zero economic growth over the last decade.

JEREMY STONE

While the Trump years slowed the progress of China's "New Economic World Order" down considerably, China is now right back to being the world's number-one exporter and producer, with a bullet. At the same time, China's growth already dominated the world economy bar none prior to 2017, the contractual five-year "scamdemic" United Nations agreement between all the nations of the world (pictured below) and their respective Central Banks played a pivotal role in shifting an already China-dominated world economy and now effectively launching it into the stratosphere. The World Economic Forum's "Great Reset" put the finishing touches on China's Economic New World Order, which at this point in time is in a virtually inexorable state from which the United States cannot recover; unless by Military force.

Communist China, a United States creation, has today -- by design, taken

TRUMP RETURNS FOR 2025

The World Bank
COVID-19 STRATEGIC PREPAREDNESS AND RESPONSE PROGRAM (SPRP) (P173789)

DATASHEET

BASIC INFORMATION

Country(ies)	Project Name	
World	COVID-19 Strategic Preparedness and Response Program (SPRP)	
Project ID	Financing Instrument	Environmental and Social Risk Classification
P173789	Investment Project Financing	Substantial

Financing & Implementation Modalities

- [✓] Multiphase Programmatic Approach (MPA)
- [ ] Series of Projects (SOP)
- [ ] Disbursement-linked Indicators (DLIs)
- [ ] Financial Intermediaries (FI)
- [ ] Project-Based Guarantee
- [ ] Deferred Drawdown
- [ ] Alternate Procurement Arrangements (APA)
- [✓] Contingent Emergency Response Component (CERC)
- [✓] Fragile State(s)
- [✓] Small State(s)
- [ ] Fragile within a non-fragile Country
- [ ] Conflict
- [✓] Responding to Natural or Man-made Disaster

Expected Project Approval Date	Expected Project Closing Date	Expected Program Closing Date
02-Apr-2020	31-Mar-2025	31-Mar-2025

complete control over the World Bank, the International Monetary Fund, and America's very own Federal Reserve Banking System. China now holds stock of 1.4 trillion in United States Treasury notes, which was sold directly to China by our very own Shadow Government! China currently holds the looming prospect of devaluing just a few of these China-owned Trillion-dollar US Treasury notes over our

JEREMY STONE

heads, making a possible World War Three look more and more like an inevitability than a "think-tank" scenario.

U.S. MILITARY

China has one military base located in Djibouti, Africa, while the United States has over 800. with unofficial operations in Libya, Western China, Tibet, Burma, Sudan, Iran, and Syria. Covering nearly every square inch of China's perimeter, comparing the Chinese Military to the United States is not worth debating. The United States Military is unquantifiably larger than China's, and for that reason alone, China has not yet utterly destroyed what is now left of American and Western Economies altogether. Without it, the U.S. and the West are sitting ducks against China's New Economic World Order. But why are there two components left that make up our New World Order to begin with? A "Military Industrial Complex" for

TRUMP RETURNS FOR 2025

America and an "Economic New World Order" for China? After all, China has had the wealth and technology to rapidly advance its Military might against the West for decades now. Have the puppet-master behind the New World Order deliberately set up a Western World's emergence without capital and money and a Chinese Government devoid of a Military? Without the noise of phony world history or a state-run propagandist media ringing in our ears, giving us implausible explanations for why this is so, it becomes noticeably clear that this lopsided New World has been set up for a future conflict between China versus the United States and the West, the likes the world has ever seen before.

JEREMY STONE
THE "MADE IN CHINA 2025', "AGENDA 2030", AND PRESIDENT TRUMP'S 2025-2029 CONNECTION

In order to adequately explain the connection and correlation between the United Nations' "Agenda 2030" (which is also nothing more than another "Red Corporate" contractual agreement between nations), "Made in China 2025" Internationalist contract, the "Pandemic's" World Bank contract (which is set to expire on Mar 31, 2025, and President Trump's return to the world's stage as the 47th President of the United States during the four-year period from 2025 through 2029, we must recognize the three core elements which each of these events has in common. The first parallel between these four events should be somewhat apparent at a glance, that being that all of these events occur between the years 2025 and 2030. The second correlation between these

TRUMP RETURNS FOR 2025

pivotal world events is that they all deal with the development of China's "New World Economic Order." The third correlation and connection between every one of these global events is much more subtle and not nearly as conspicuous as the first two; that is that they are all signed as business contracts or "Red Corporate" partnerships between Nations, and not the historically used "treaties" one would expect to find between World Governments. Although the verbiage between the words "contract" and "treaty" has similarities on the surface, these two words mean two entirely different things. They suggest that China's New World Order's recently enhanced addition is run more like a Corporation than a Government.

"The nerds are running the show in today's China. In the twenty years since Deng Xiaoping's reforms kicked in, the

JEREMY STONE

composition of the Chinese leadership has shifted markedly in favor of technocrats. ...It's no exaggeration to describe the current regime as a technocracy. After the Maoist madness abated and Deng Xiaoping inaugurated the opening and reforms that began in late 1978, scientific and technical intellectuals were among the first to be rehabilitated. Realizing that they were the key to the Four Modernizations embraced by the reformers, concerted efforts were made to bring the "experts" back into the fold. During the 1980s, technocracy as a concept was much talked about, especially in the context of so-called "Neo-Authoritarianism" — the principle at the heart of the "Asian Developmental Model" that South Korea, Singapore, and Taiwan had pursued with apparent success. The basic beliefs and assumptions of the technocrats were laid out quite plainly: Social and economic problems were akin to engineering problems and could be under-

TRUMP RETURNS FOR 2025

stood, addressed, and eventually solved as such." – **from "The Revenge of the Nerds: China had been converted into a Technocracy!" – Time Magazine**

Although the agendas behind the U.N's "Agenda 2030", the World Bank's Pandemic I.N.C.'s expiration date - set for 2025., and Communist China's "Made in China 2025" agenda may seem independent from one another, they have been pre-staged and calculated

JEREMY STONE

meticulously, solely to bolster Communist China's absolute New World Order.

The global elite has disguised the superficial definition of the United Nation's agenda to mean "a permanent reduction of "humankind's" carbon footprint," which is just a crafty way of misconstruing its true agenda; which is THE PERMANENT REDUCTION OF MANKIND'S NATURAL RESOURCES – THE DEPRIVATION OF THE ENERGY AND RESOURCES USED IN NATURAL GAS/OIL, WATER, HUMAN REPRODUCTION (BABIES/A.K.A. "HUMAN RESOURCES"), OUR FOOD SUPPLY, AND EVEN THE AIR WE BREATHE! In short, agenda 2030 is, in reality, more than just a deadline for a Green New Hoaxed World. It has been constructed by the United Nations as the ultimate tool to create the illusion that China holds what little is left of the world's natural resources, so we all must

TRUMP RETURNS FOR 2025

take care not to squander mother earth's dwindling supply on ourselves. The scarcity of the Earth's natural resources is one of the world's most significant lies ever told. Not only is there no shortages, now or to come of any of the world's resources, but the scarcity of oil is one of the oldest surviving lies on Earth, famously perpetrated by the New World Order's founder, John Rockefeller, who coined the term "fossil fuel" to create the illusion that oil was as rare and old as rotting dinosaurs, when oil is, in fact, as abundant as freshwater throughout the world. This same, now antiquated idea to make the Earth's natural resources found in abundance appear scarce to maximize profits for the elite while eliminating the poor and middle-class is being used to hoax society into believing food, energy, water, and air are in short supply: and that China must step in to decide how to regulate what is left of our "dying planet properly."

JEREMY STONE

"Made in China 2025" is not a slogan to promote Chinese-made goods. It is a globalized contract made with the World Bank, International Monetary Fund, and the 4th Reich's (European-based) World Economic Forum who struck a deal with China-based Red Corporate Organizations in an effort to capitalize on the "pandemic." The testing, the vaccinations, the medical facilities, and yes, the pharmaceutical companies with American names are in reality China-owned and are all profiting for the betterment of a totalitarian-run One-World Government and newly realized China-run New World Order. And when do you suppose both "Made in China 2025" and pandemic contract are set to complete with an expiration date? Again, not coincidentally, they both expire on Mar 31, 2025. By this time, China will have complete domination over the Governments and Corporations of the world at large.

TRUMP RETURNS FOR 2025

Yet, there is another strange twist to this historical saga between East and West. By Mar 31, 2025, as China reaches the completion of its One-World Government and an even more distorted New World Order than the previous American/British Imperialist; Trump will be exactly 39 days into his second term as the 47th President of the United States, creating the conditions for the 'perfect storm' and the inevitable final showdown for survival between the United States and China.

While the internationalist elite have intentionally shaped the dualist nature of our current lopsided New World Order, pitting both the Military-dominate United States VS the Economic-dominate Chinese C.C.P. against one another, the prototypical and expected response to these manufactured chain of events would be a "globalized synthesis" between Communist and Capitalist

JEREMY STONE

worlds; but under the coming Trump Presidency, a synthesized Communist/Capitalist world merger becomes an impossibility, as intensive negotiations and deal-making between nations over which side to take during a possible World War Three scenario becomes the only sensible possibility left for world stability within our current system built upon "New World Disorder."

TRUMP RETURNS FOR 2025

JEREMY STONE

TRUMP RETURNS FOR 2025

JEREMY STONE

TRUMP RETURNS FOR 2025

Issue #1 — June 10, 2021

JEREMY STONE

TRUTH

HIDDEN HISTORY + DEEP STATE EXPOSED + AGENDAS REVEALED

9/11 NUCLEAR DEMOLITION?
EXPOSING THE UNTOLD HARD TRUTH BEHIND SEPTEMBER 11TH, 2001

Will Trump Make America Great Again in 2024?

MAN OF THE YEAR

The Return of Hybids & Nephilim Recovered

Trump's Top 20 accomplishments while in office

www.Deepstatebooks.com

Be sure to check out my new monthly magazine, "Truth" –

JEREMY STONE

Available at www.DeepStateBooks.com and Amazon coming June 10th!

TRUMP RETURNS FOR 2025

JEREMY STONE

TRUMP RETURNS FOR 2025

JEREMY STONE

TRUMP RETURNS FOR 2025

JEREMY STONE

TRUMP RETURNS FOR 2025

JEREMY STONE

TRUMP RETURNS FOR 2025

JEREMY STONE

Made in the USA
Middletown, DE
16 July 2021